LEARN BY STICKER®

More Addition & Subtraction

workman

· NEW YORK ·

Workman Kids
Workman Publishing
Hachette Book Group, Inc.
1290 Avenue of the Americas
New York, NY 10104
workman.com

Workman Kids is an imprint of Workman Publishing, a division of Hachette Book Group, Inc. LEARN BY STICKER and the Workman name and logo are registered trademarks of Hachette Book Group, Inc.

Design by Ying Cheng and Lourdes Ubidia
The 10 low-poly images in this book are based on illustrations by Ying Cheng.
Activity illustrations by Lourdes Ubidia
Concept by Alisha Zucker
Text by Katie Campbell

The publisher is not responsible for websites (or their content) that are not owned by the publisher.

Workman books may be purchased in bulk for business, educational, or promotional use. For information, please contact your local bookseller or the Hachette Book Group Special Markets Department at special.markets@hbgusa.com.

ISBN 978-1-5235-2424-2
First Edition May 2024 APS

Distributed in Europe by Hachette Livre, 58 rue Jean Bleuzen, 92 178 Vanves Cedex, France.

Distributed in the United Kingdom by Hachette Book Group, UK, Carmelite House, 50 Victoria Embankment, London EC4Y 0DZ.

Printed in China on responsibly sourced paper.

10 9 8 7 6 5 4 3 2 1

HOW TO LEARN BY STICKER®

1. SOLVE IN ORDER. Sticker maps for each fantasy animal are in the front of the book. Math concepts build on one another, so complete the pages in order!

Sticker map

2. FIND YOUR STICKERS. Sticker sheets for each picture are in the back of the book. Use the image in the top right corner of each sticker sheet to find the one that matches the picture. Both the sticker map and sticker sheet can be torn out of the book, so you don't have to flip back and forth between them.

Sticker sheet

3. DO THE MATH! Solve the math problem and write the answer in the box. Then match the answer and color of the problem to the number and color on the sticker sheet. Each sticker matches only one space on the sticker map. Place each sticker in the matching space on the sticker map. Be careful! The stickers aren't removable.

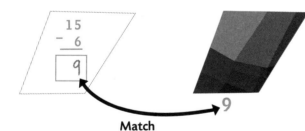

$$\begin{array}{r} 15 \\ -6 \\ \hline 9 \end{array}$$

9

Match

Finished picture

4. TURN THE PAGE. There are fun math activities on the back of each picture to get extra practice and strengthen your math skills.

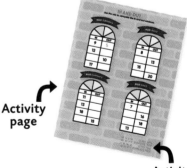

Activity page

Activity answers

LET'S SOLVE AND STICKER!

Directions

Addition through 20
Fill in the missing numbers to complete the addition problems.

Adding 10s
Fill in the missing numbers to complete the addition problems.

Subtraction within 20
Fill in the missing numbers to complete the subtraction problems.

Subtracting 10s
Fill in the missing numbers to complete the subtraction problems.

Addition and Subtraction within 20
Fill in the missing numbers to complete the addition and subtraction problems.

Adding and Subtracting 10s
Fill in the missing numbers to complete the addition and subtraction problems.

Skip Counting by 2s and 5s
Fill in the missing numbers to skip count by 2s or 5s.

Addition through 100
Fill in the missing numbers to complete the addition problems.

Skip Counting by 10s
Fill in the missing numbers to skip count by 10s.

Subtraction within 100
Fill in the missing numbers to complete the subtraction problems.

$+\dfrac{\boxed{}}{10}$ ← with **1** above

$\boxed{} + 10 = 20$

$+\dfrac{4}{4}$ with $\boxed{}$ below

$\dfrac{+\ 4}{15}$ with $\boxed{}$ above

$+\dfrac{6}{6}$ with $\boxed{}$ below

9 $+\dfrac{\boxed{}}{15}$

7 $+\dfrac{\boxed{}}{14}$

$\dfrac{+\ 13}{20}$ with $\boxed{}$ above

$10 + 1 = \boxed{}$

$+\dfrac{3}{4}$ with $\boxed{}$ below

$17 + 3 = \boxed{}$

$+\dfrac{5}{17}$ with $\boxed{}$

$\dfrac{+\ 10}{19}$ with $\boxed{}$ above

$\dfrac{+\ 2}{10}$ with $\boxed{}$ above

$+\dfrac{12}{4}$ with $\boxed{}$ below

$5 + 15 = \boxed{}$

$11 + 2 = \boxed{}$

$+\dfrac{10}{18}$ with $\boxed{}$

$3 + \boxed{} = 14$

$6 + 4 = \boxed{}$

RIDDLE

Solve the equations on the lily pads. Then write the letters on the matching blank lines to solve the riddle.

O
3 + 7 = ___

N
6 + 13 = ___

R
11 + 3 = ___

U
8 + 8 = ___

I
6 + 5 = ___

E
5 + 12 = ___

B
11 + 9 = ___

T
3 + 10 = ___

Y
13 + 2 = ___

What do you get when you add a frog and a rabbit?

___ ___ ___ ___ ___ ___ ___ ___ ___ ___ ___ ___ ___ ___!
10 19 17   20 16 19 19 15   14 11 20 20 11 13

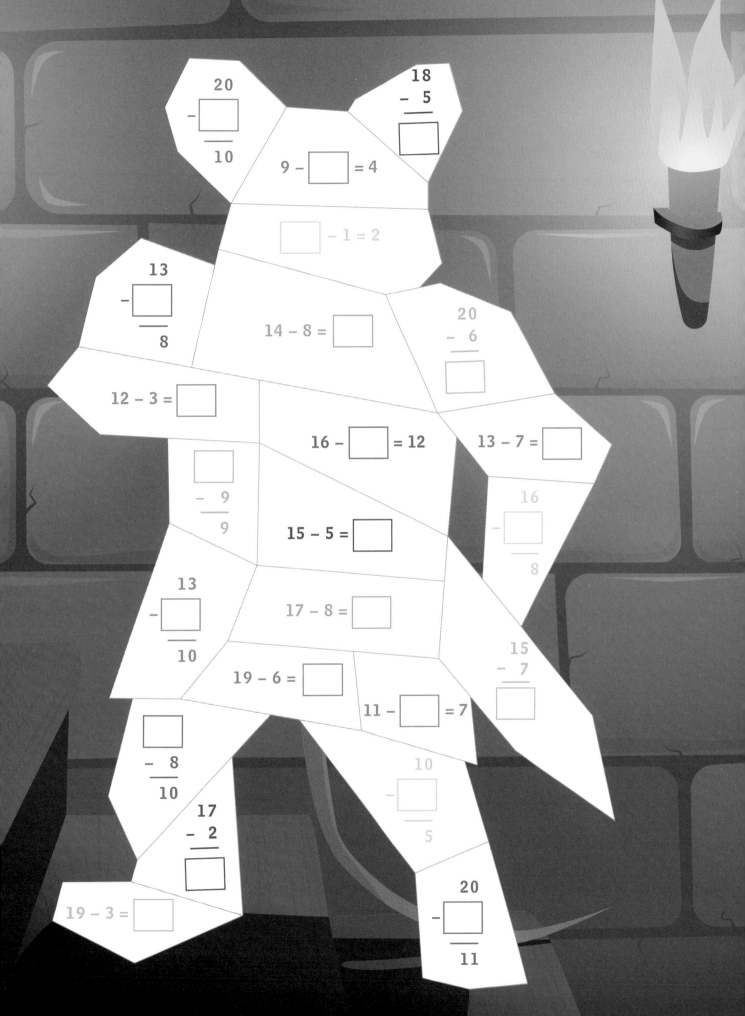

SUBTRACTION WHEELS

Subtract the blue numbers from the **black** number
in the center to complete the cheese wheels.

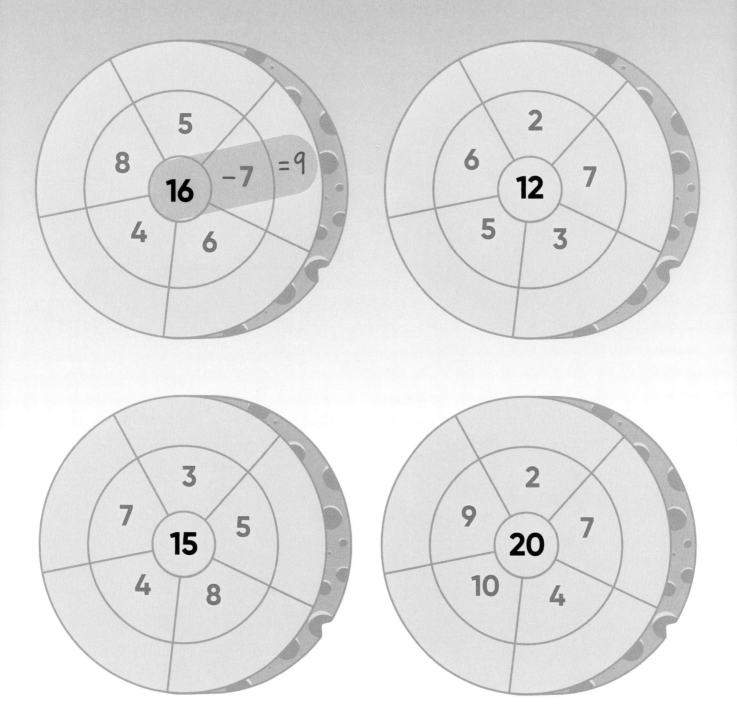

IN AND OUT

Use the rule to complete the in and out windows.

RULE: Subtract 4

IN	OUT
9	5
12	
	10
17	

RULE: Add 3

IN	OUT
8	
	13
15	
	20

RULE: Subtract 5

IN	OUT
11	
13	
18	
	15

RULE: Add 7

IN	OUT
7	
	16
	18
13	

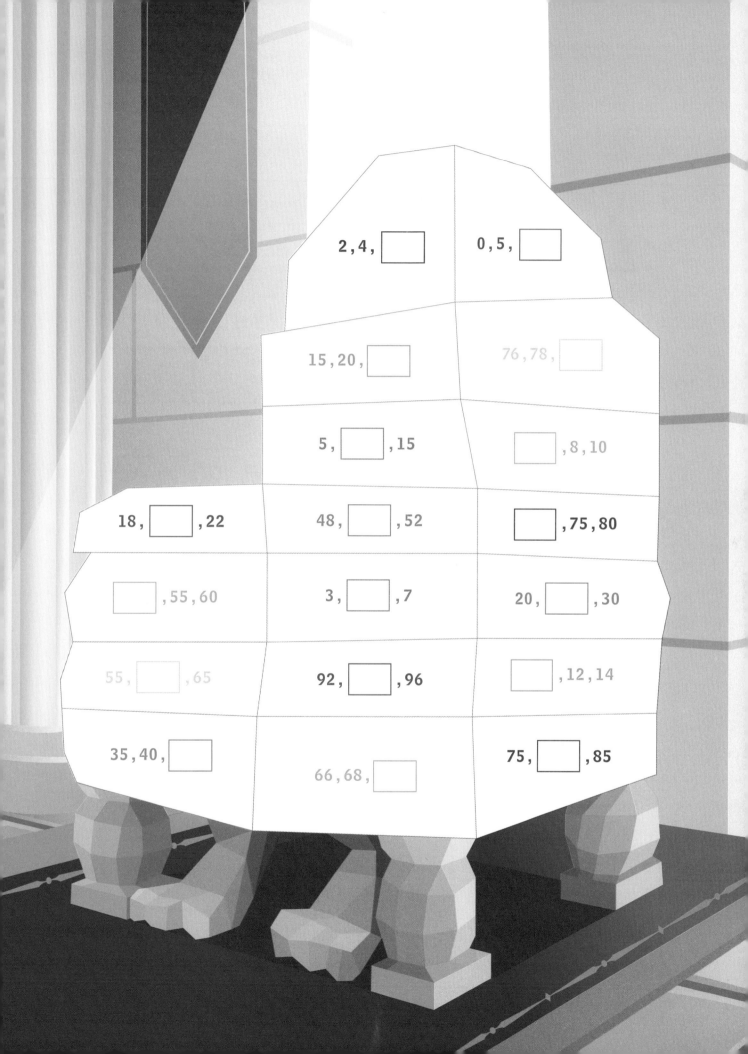

2, 4, ☐

0, 5, ☐

15, 20, ☐

76, 78, ☐

5, ☐, 15

☐, 8, 10

18, ☐, 22

48, ☐, 52

☐, 75, 80

☐, 55, 60

3, ☐, 7

20, ☐, 30

55, ☐, 65

92, ☐, 96

☐, 12, 14

35, 40, ☐

66, 68, ☐

75, ☐, 85

SKIP COUNTING

Skip count by 2 or 5 and write the missing numbers to complete each sequence.

12 | ___ | ___ | 18 | ___

___ | 35 | ___ | 45 | ___

___ | 58 | ___ | 62 | ___

75 | ___ | ___ | ___ | 95

14, 16, 20
30, 40, 50
56, 60, 64
80, 85, 90

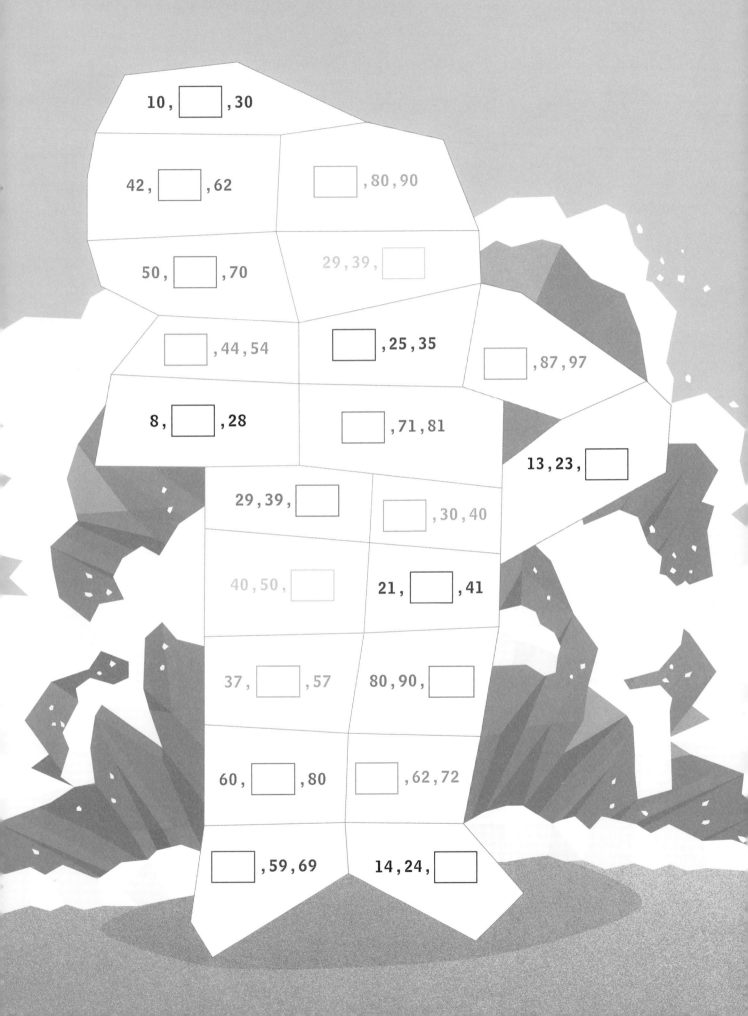

FOLLOW THE PATHS

King Frog and Sir Mouse are walking home through the enchanted forest.
Frog starts at 5 and skip counts by 10 to move. Color Frog's path blue.
Mouse starts at 17 and skip counts by 10 to move. Color Mouse's path red.

FROG START

FROG HOME

MOUSE HOME

MOUSE START

5	15	30	40	50	55	120	110	100
10	25	35	45	52	60	130	145	155
15	30	40	55	54	65	75	135	145
20	50	60	65	75	85	90	125	130
35	70	77	87	97	95	105	115	120
40	50	67	70	107	100	110	120	110
45	47	57	100	117	127	137	160	165
22	37	42	105	102	135	147	157	167
17	27	32	110	107	140	150	155	160

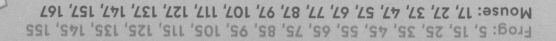

Frog: 5, 15, 25, 35, 45, 55, 65, 75, 85, 95, 105, 115, 125, 135, 145, 155
Mouse: 17, 27, 37, 47, 57, 67, 77, 87, 97, 107, 117, 127, 137, 147, 157, 167

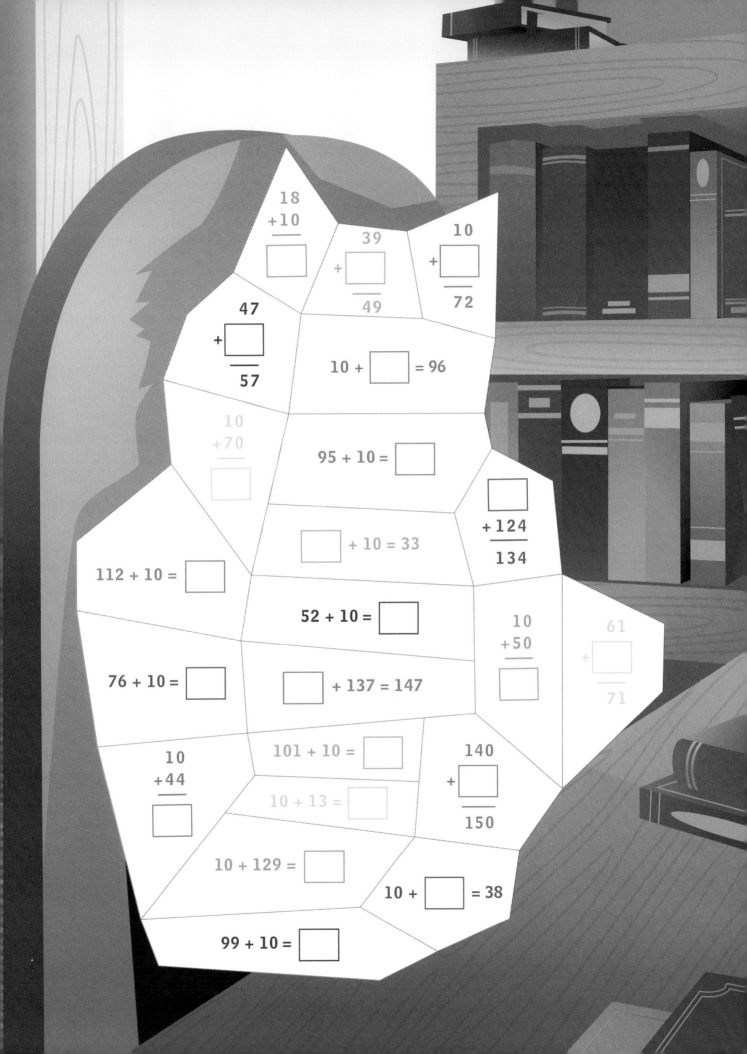

18
$+10$
☐

39
$+$ ☐
49

10
$+$ ☐
72

47
$+$ ☐
57

$10 +$ ☐ $= 96$

10
$+70$
☐

$95 + 10 =$ ☐

☐
$+124$
134

☐ $+ 10 = 33$

$112 + 10 =$ ☐

$52 + 10 =$ ☐

10
$+50$
☐

61
$+$ ☐
71

$76 + 10 =$ ☐

☐ $+ 137 = 147$

10
$+44$
☐

$101 + 10 =$ ☐

$10 + 13 =$ ☐

140
$+$ ☐
150

$10 + 129 =$ ☐

$10 +$ ☐ $= 38$

$99 + 10 =$ ☐

DECODING SHAPES

Each shape represents a number. Use the
given numbers to solve for the missing values.

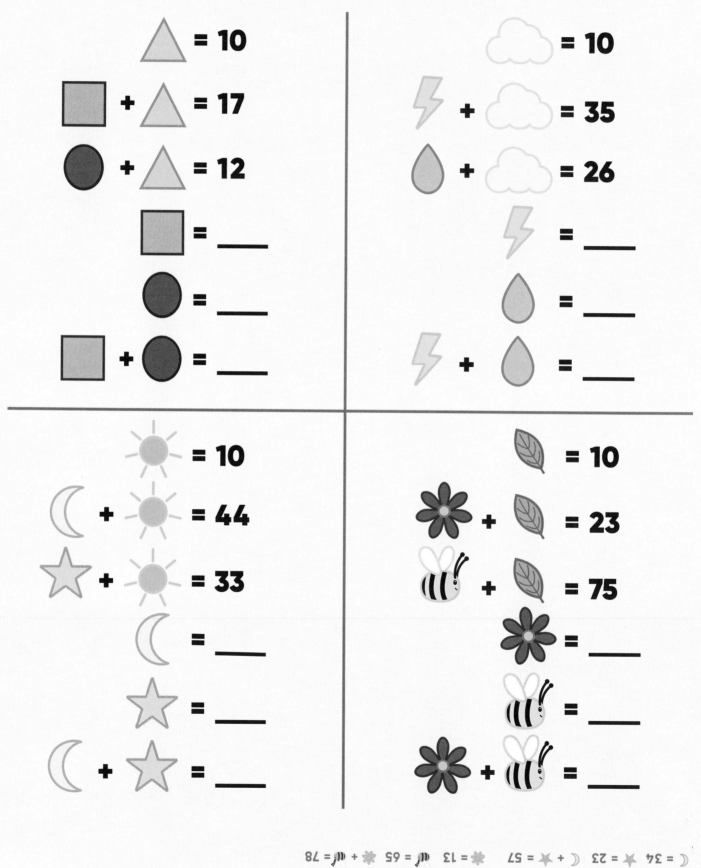

△ = 10

■ + △ = 17

● + △ = 12

■ = ____

● = ____

■ + ● = ____

☁ = 10

⚡ + ☁ = 35

💧 + ☁ = 26

⚡ = ____

💧 = ____

⚡ + 💧 = ____

☀ = 10

🌙 + ☀ = 44

⭐ + ☀ = 33

🌙 = ____

⭐ = ____

🌙 + ⭐ = ____

🍃 = 10

🌼 + 🍃 = 23

🐝 + 🍃 = 75

🌼 = ____

🐝 = ____

🌼 + 🐝 = ____

$$21 - \boxed{} = 11$$

$$40 - 10 = \boxed{}$$

$$27 - 10 = \boxed{}$$

$$125 - \boxed{} = 115$$

$$73 - 10 = \boxed{}$$

$$104 - 10 = \boxed{}$$

$$\boxed{} - 10 = 20$$

$$88 - 10 = \boxed{}$$

$$76 - 10 = \boxed{}$$

$$51 - 10 = \boxed{}$$

$$125 - \boxed{} = 115$$

$$60 - 10 = \boxed{}$$

$$32 - \boxed{} = 22$$

$$99 - 10 = \boxed{}$$

$$39 - 10 = \boxed{}$$

$$109 - 10 = \boxed{}$$

$$101 - 10 = \boxed{}$$

$$\boxed{} - 10 = 53$$

$$77 - \boxed{} = 67$$

$$96 - \boxed{} = 86$$

$$54 - 10 = \boxed{}$$

$$45 - \boxed{} = 35$$

RIDDLE

Solve the equations. Then write the letters on the matching blanks.

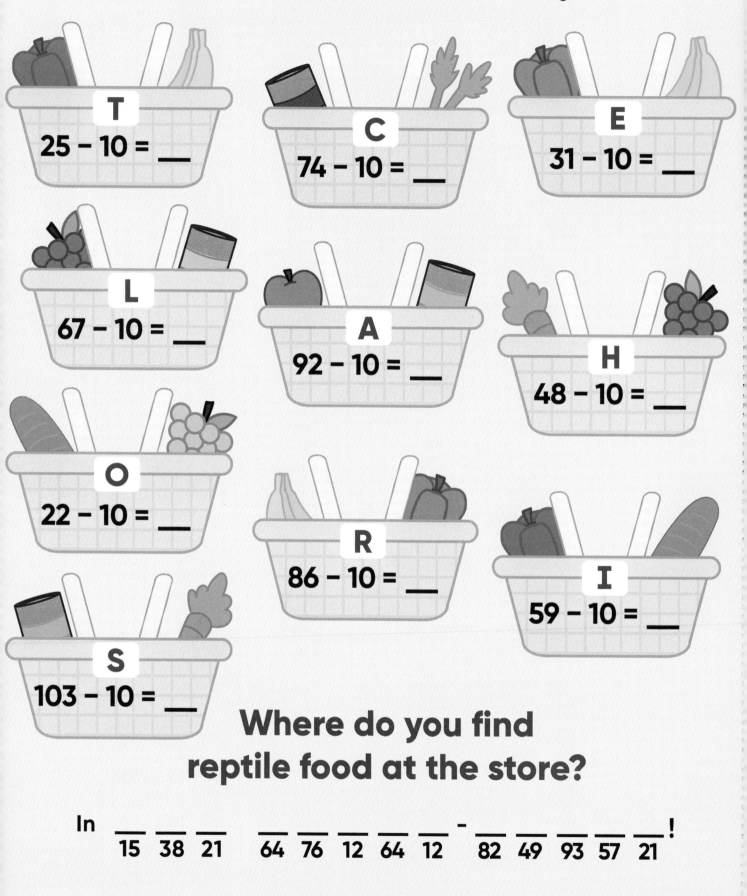

T 25 – 10 = ___

C 74 – 10 = ___

E 31 – 10 = ___

L 67 – 10 = ___

A 92 – 10 = ___

H 48 – 10 = ___

O 22 – 10 = ___

R 86 – 10 = ___

I 59 – 10 = ___

S 103 – 10 = ___

Where do you find reptile food at the store?

In ___ ___ ___   ___ ___ ___ ___ ___ - ___ ___ ___ ___ ___ !
15 38 21   64 76 12 64 12   82 49 93 57 21

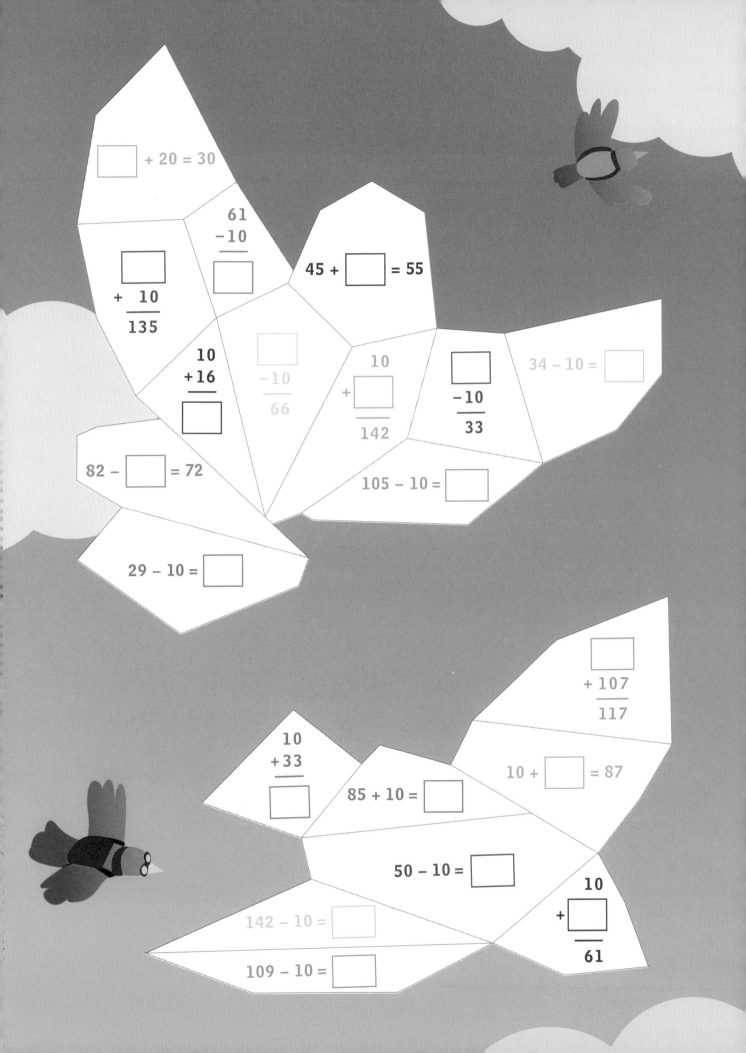

$\boxed{} + 20 = 30$

$\begin{array}{r} 61 \\ -10 \\ \hline \boxed{} \end{array}$

$\begin{array}{r} \boxed{} \\ +\ 10 \\ \hline 135 \end{array}$

$45 + \boxed{} = 55$

$\begin{array}{r} 10 \\ +16 \\ \hline \boxed{} \end{array}$

$\begin{array}{r} \boxed{} \\ -10 \\ \hline 66 \end{array}$

$\begin{array}{r} 10 \\ + \boxed{} \\ \hline 142 \end{array}$

$\begin{array}{r} \boxed{} \\ -10 \\ \hline 33 \end{array}$

$34 - 10 = \boxed{}$

$82 - \boxed{} = 72$

$105 - 10 = \boxed{}$

$29 - 10 = \boxed{}$

$\begin{array}{r} \boxed{} \\ +107 \\ \hline 117 \end{array}$

$\begin{array}{r} 10 \\ +33 \\ \hline \boxed{} \end{array}$

$85 + 10 = \boxed{}$

$10 + \boxed{} = 87$

$50 - 10 = \boxed{}$

$\begin{array}{r} 10 \\ + \boxed{} \\ \hline 61 \end{array}$

$142 - 10 = \boxed{}$

$109 - 10 = \boxed{}$

MORE AND LESS

Fill in the missing numbers to complete the puzzles.

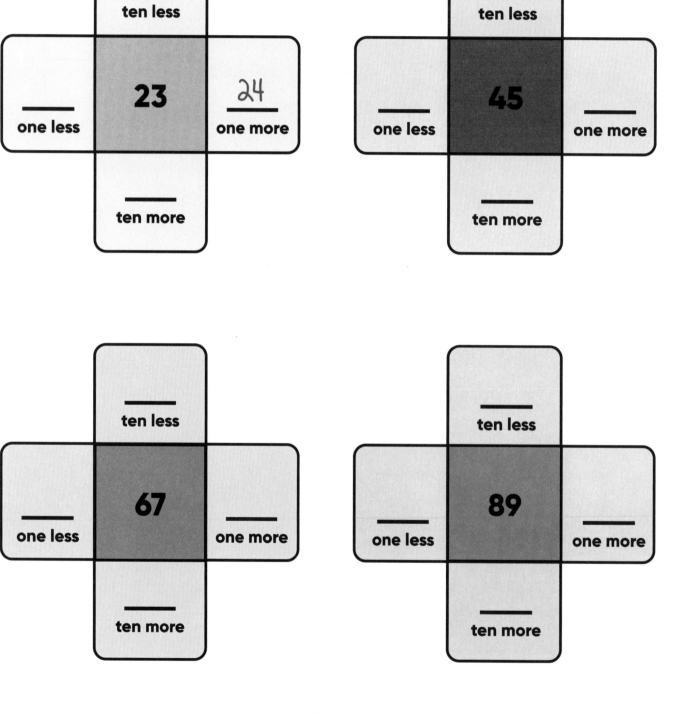

23

- 13 ten less
- ___ one less
- 24 one more
- ___ ten more

45

- ___ ten less
- ___ one less
- ___ one more
- ___ ten more

67

- ___ ten less
- ___ one less
- ___ one more
- ___ ten more

89

- ___ ten less
- ___ one less
- ___ one more
- ___ ten more

23 one less = 22, one more = 24, ten less = 13, ten more = 33
45 one less = 44, one more = 46, ten less = 35, ten more = 55
67 one less = 66, one more = 68, ten less = 57, ten more = 77
89 one less = 88, one more = 90, ten less = 79, ten more = 99

ADDITION PYRAMIDS

Each number in the pyramid is the sum of the two numbers below it.
Add the numbers to find the missing sums.

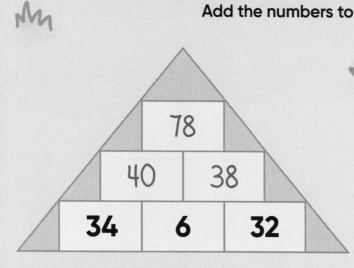

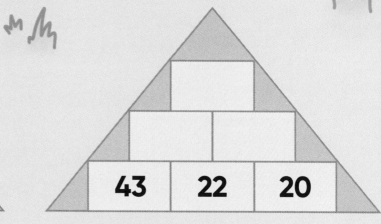

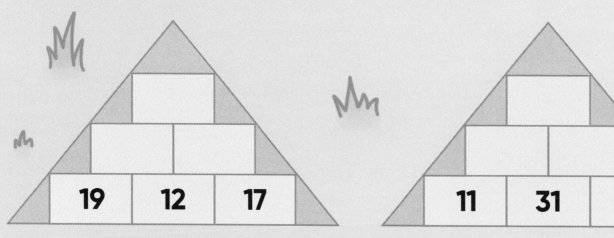

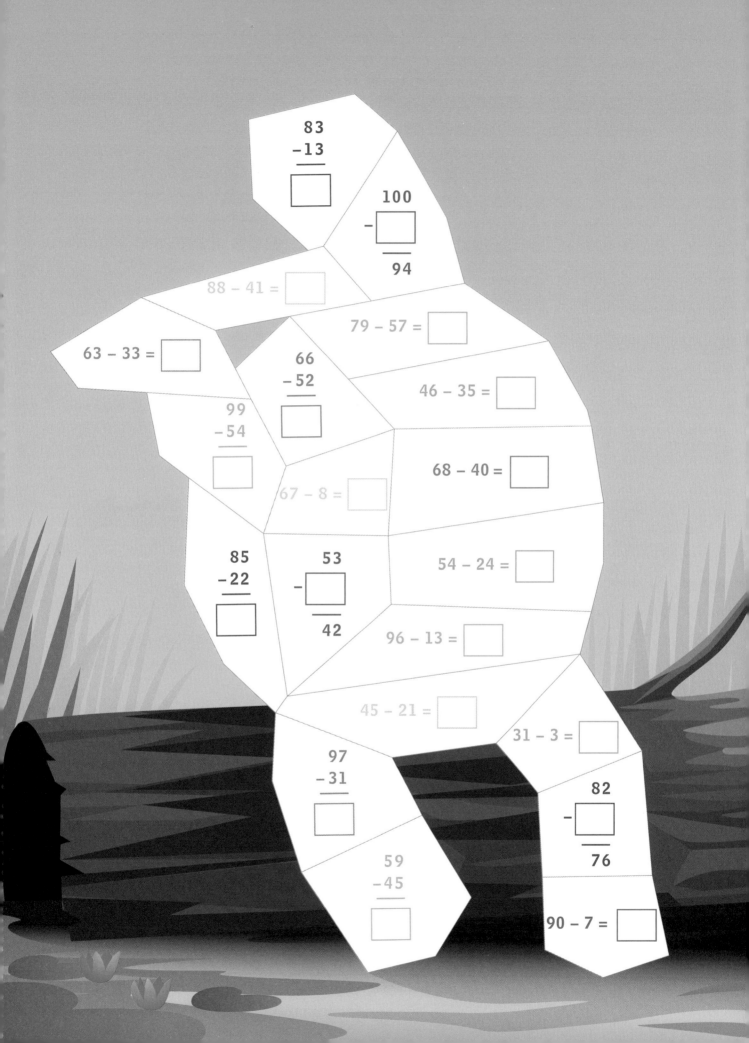

CONCERT TIME!

Solve the problems. The turtle can only travel on steps that have a 3 in the answer. Color the path the turtle should take to the stage.

21
− 8

89
− 26

28
− 12

54
− 6

68
− 25

97
− 63

78
− 41

52
− 40

76
− 25

45
− 9